Emotions of a

Lifetime

Emotions of a Lifetime is written by Dolores R. Fitzpatrick
Copyright 2005, Dolores R. Fitzpatrick

Published and Printed by:
    Lifevest Publishing
    4901 E. Dry Creek Road, #170
    Centennial, CO 80122
    www.lifevestpublishing.com

Printed in the United States of America

I.S.B.N. 1-59879-075-7

Emotions
of a
Lifetime

Dolores R. Fitzpatrick

**This book is dedicated to my mother:
Delia Rose Mahon Fitzpatrick
1937 - 2001**

Thank you for giving me all the love, support, encouragement and strength my heart could hold. It is both an honor and privilege to have you for my mom. I miss you more than I could ever express. May your Heavenly ears hear the words I have written on these pages. Until we meet again face to face, I take comfort in knowing you are with me always.

I Love You!

Acknowledgments

Susan - Thank you for all your support, encouragement and help. Your pictures brighten the pages of this book just as you brighten the lives of so many.

My Family - Thank you for your unconditional love and unyielding support.

All my angels... both on this earth and in Heaven. Thank you for watching over me and allowing me to feel your presence.

All my "editors"... you know who you are. Thank you for your advice and input.

**To all who touch
my life
and become my
inspiration**

Like Mom

I look in the mirror and see your face a
little more each day
I reach to grab something and get a
glimpse of my hands only to realize
they are your hands which I held so
very often
Words flow from my mouth and before
I can even comprehend it
I hear your voice

I am part of you and you are with
me always
A little more like you each day…
And Mom I really love it

Enjoy

No matter where I am or what

I'm doing I always try to keep one

thing in mind

This is the only life you're gonna have

Live it well…and enjoy!

Know My Love

How can I tell you how much
I love you
Do I say it with words and hope they
come out right
Do I say it with actions and hope you
see the meaning behind them
Do I sit quietly and hold you
and hope that you feel my love

To do any single one of these

would not be enough

So I will do all of them and hope

you know my love

A Wonderful Gift

The swaying trees

The warm breeze on my face

The rays of sun beating down

The smell of flowers

The sound of children playing and

dogs barking

The blue sky with white puffy clouds

All of these things I experience simply

because I exist

Isn't life a wonderful gift

Without Reason

As I sit staring out over the water
I think of the way things once were
and how I would like them to be
Always there for me when I needed
you but now no longer around
Was it something I did or said
that made you leave or was it a
battle inside yourself
Always there to share the good and
bad now gone without a reason

I guess it's time to pull myself back
together and go on with my life
If only I knew what made you
leave like you did it would be so
much easier
But instead of asking questions
I cannot answer I'll think of all the
good times we had together
Instead of worrying about why
you left I'll just be happy that for a
short time we were able to share
our lives

Alone In A Crowd

I stand alone and prepare my mind

My body is well trained and ready

to face the challenge

The long hours spent preparing for

this moment

The time has come to recite what

I've learned

Every step, every thought, with one

goal in mind

I stand alone and prepare my

mind…in a crowd of thousands

My Promise

I have not much to give you for I

am not rich with possessions

Sometimes I feel as if you deserve

much more than I am able to give

Although I'm not able to shower

you with material things

I am able to promise you this…

I will give you all the love

your heart can hold

And I will care for you

like no one has before

Material things can come and go

but my love will last forever

Dreamer

Look into the eyes of a dreamer
and you'll see a mind full of
possibilities

A Certain Look

Lately when I look at you

I see a look of concern which in

turn concerns me

You tell me that I'm acting

differently than I used to

Changing my moods much too

quickly and frequently

I tell you there's nothing to worry

about

Yet you still have that look in your

eyes

Please believe what I tell you

Don't worry about me

Let me handle things myself

But if I may ask one favor of you

Please don't look at me with

concern

Instead look at me with

confidence

Early Morning Peace

To rise while the world is still

sleeping

My footsteps transcending the

stillness of predawn

The quiet streets become my

personal freedom

Free to run and truly think

Nothing but my footsteps breaking

the silence

Oh how I love the early morning

peace

Faith

Someday I'll see you again and all
will be clear
All the pain, suffering and sadness
will finally make sense
I'll have the answers to all the
questions
that run through my mind

There's plenty I don't understand

But I guess that's what faith is

Accepting that things happen for a

reason even when I just don't

understand

We Are All One

Nothing brings people closer
together than working toward one
common goal
Wouldn't it be nice if we could
make the world's common goal
to have everyone act as one

The True Strength

The strength which comes from my
body is nothing more than muscle
mass
The strength which comes from my
mind is nothing more than brain
power

But the strength which comes from

my heart gives meaning to my

existence

Differences

The differences in people

are beyond compare

All races, ages and genders together

for what seems so long but is really

just a moment in the sphere of life

To remain within my own reality

is to miss out on the vastness of

humanity

They Matter To Me

It's true I'm going through a
tough time right now
Things aren't really going as
planned
I figure I've probably just set my
goals too high
But I'm not going to give up
I'm going to keep climbing until
I reach them

You say I'm a dreamer and

I need to start living in reality

Well my dreams are reality to me

and they will materialize

with time

I don't expect you to understand my

goals

But I would like you to

understand how important they are

to me

Grateful

The pavement beneath my feet

My home away from home

It tests the limits of my mind, body

and soul

To go deep within myself and come

out a stronger person

How grateful I am to feel my heart

pump, my legs ache and my brow

sweat

How many would give all to have

the opportunity I have each day

Danny, Matt and Kayla

If I tried to put into words the love
I hold for you
The sweetest, kindest, most loving
words, still would never do
I look at you with wonder and
with a grateful heart
You've brought such joy and
happiness to my life
right from the start
And if I may just tell you
another thing or two

I'll be here for you always

Forever this is true

My love is unconditional and shall

last your whole life through

No aunt could ever have more love

than what I have for you

Tree Of Life

To see a tree standing strong and tall
To know that it has weathered
many storms
To feel its strength within my eyes
And know its power within my soul
For I can relate so well to this
mighty structure
Strong when needed
Yet always flexible to weather
the storms of life

A Place In My Heart

It started with a phone call… the

emptiness that is

The words I knew would come one day

but a shock nonetheless

A place in my heart put aside just

for you

No longer will it be filled with

happy times of the present

I must now keep it for memories

of the past

I guess the empty feeling comes

during the period of time in which

I realize there will be no more

memories made

And I begin to recall what we

once shared

Grandma - I Love You!

To Answer Myself

What others think or do not think

is none of my concern

For my concern lies only in my

own mind

Need I answer to anyone but

myself...I think not

But to not answer myself honestly

would prove to be treacherous

My Goal Is You

As I sit and try to write about all
that you mean to me I seem to get
lost in my emotions
You're everything I've ever dreamed of
Everything I could ever want in love
You take my fears and ever so
gently caress them away
You listen to what I have to say
and to what I cannot say except
with my heart

You help me to know myself and in

you I found what true love is

A love which engulfs every emotion

and every thought I could ever have

What I want for us is simple

I want us to be "us" forever

I need to work many things out

within myself

But I know that being with you is

my ultimate goal

If I can keep myself focused on you

I will no doubt be able to

overcome any obstacle

From Dark To Light

You enter and turn my world from
gray to bright yellow
Once a dark cloud masked over by
laughter
Now a bright sun with no need to
hide

Lifetime Friend

Two years went by so very fast

and are now about to end

I wish nothing but the best for you

my very special friend

I never thought when we first met

we would become as close as this

Now I find myself so often saying

that it's you I'm gonna miss

Our friendship's grown and

strengthened through the good

times and the bad

That's why I know that when you leave

I will be very sad

I know I'll shed a tear or two when

you turn to go away

But a part of me will go with you

and a part of you will stay

As we go our separate ways we must

go with thoughts so fond

Because no time nor distance

could ever break our bond

And though we say "good-bye" for

now we know it's not the end

Because you see we've truly found the

meaning of "lifetime friend"

As You Sleep

Upon your face the morning light
shines
You sleep with the calmness of a
baby
All the problems of the day before
are forgotten in the darkness of the
night
You wake with a jump and look around
just long enough to ensure
yourself it was only a
dream

Time For Myself

Time for myself doesn't always
come along as often as I would like
There's always something to do,
someone to see
or somewhere to go
Sometimes I wish I could freeze
time just long enough to have a few
minutes to myself and get my
thoughts together

Unfortunately time just won't
stand still
So I guess I'll just have to do my
best to find time for myself even when
I'm not by myself

Knowing Myself

People say that they know me and
that I'm so easy to read
When I hear these words
I just have to laugh
How can others know me when
I don't even know myself

Remember What Was

I can't remember what it was like
to live without you in my life
The pain of all that loneliness now
gently seems to fade
But to not remember it at all
would not be very wise
For if I completely forget the life of
loneliness which I have left behind
there will remain no means of
comparison

And if I fail to compare then and
now, I may take now for
granted

Time For Change

At this point in my life I'm content

to:

-get up in the morning

-put in a day's work

-come home

-eat

-sleep

and start it all over again

the next morning

That's how I know it's time

for a change

Too Beautiful For Words

The words "I love you" cannot

begin to express what you mean to me

For these words merely scratch the

surface of my feelings and emotions

Words alone could not describe what

you have added to my life

In you I have found the person with

whom I want to share everything

including my future

You give me your love and ask for

nothing in return

With you I have found what true

happiness is

Not a day goes by that I don't think of

you and thank God for bringing you

into my life

You have exceeded all expectations of

what love means to me

I wish there were words I could say

to show you how deeply I have been

touched by your love

But just as a rainbow is too beautiful

for words…so too is our love

Past Is Past

Why take up so much time looking

back on your past mistakes

and bad choices

Instead use that time to

-look to the future

-plan your dreams

and live and love your life

Darkness

The darkness will come all too soon

to the life that has meant so much

to so many

A life well lived but cut down too soon

How do you tell someone who is

dying how much they mean to you

How do you say the words

while holding back the tears

For if the tears start flowing

I feel they will never stop

Trying to be strong for the sake of
another is certainly no easy task
Am I being strong for others
or for myself
Maybe if I remain strong
it won't happen

A Different Outlook

When you look at me you see

confidence, strength and

independence

But when I look at myself

those qualities seem to change

I see my weaknesses and

insecurities

Maybe the world would seem brighter

if I learned to think like

you

Live And Dream

Life goes on but I don't live it

Life is good but I can't feel it

Life is there but I can't see it

For I'm so caught up in a world

where everything is routine

It's the same thing day in/day out

I do the same things

I see the same people

I go the same places

If I could just take a day to stop

and look and listen

If I could just take a day to get

reacquainted with the person I am

But time for this does not come easily

I may not have the time but

I'll have to make it

So many things are important in this

life

but do not fall into our

everyday routines

For this reason we must make the

time to live and even dream

Quiet Times

Quiet times of boredom:

-time to think, plan, dream

Time to step inside myself and think

in terms of "me"

Then you enter and all that changes

Quiet times of boredom…now replaced

by thoughts of you

Stop And See

As I sit and look out the window

I notice things which I never

before really stopped to appreciate

Not only were my eyes opened

but my ears as well

Many people take these things for

granted and in doing so miss out on

an important part of life

- the turning leaves

- the sun shining through the trees

- the bright blue sky

- the birds flying high -

- the sound of people and planes and

cars which can be heard both

near and far

These are just a few of the beautiful

things which many people never

stop to look at and listen to

I've found that life means much

more to me if I take the time to

stop and see all the beautiful things

God put here for me

The sun, a bird, a flower, a tree

Every Step

I once ran alone even when

amongst others

It's something that runners do

We run to think, to feel, to enjoy

and sometimes even to forget

I will never again run alone

You will always be right there

You left this world in a physical sense

and now your soul is within me

with every step I take

My Puppy

You give such love and sweet affection

and ask for nothing in return

It's love in just its purest form

From you, people could learn

So happy just to be with me and

lie there at my feet

To have you in my life has been a

very special treat

I've raised you from a few weeks old

We've been through quite a lot

And when your running slows a bit

Along with you I'll trot

You may be getting older now

but in my heart you'll stay

That little, tiny puppy dog that

I brought home that day

To Order Copies of

Emotions of a

Lifetime

by **Dolores R. Fitzpatrick**

I.S.B.N. 1-59879-075-7

Order Online at:
www.authorstobelievein.com

By Phone Toll Free at:
1-877-843-1007

By Mail:
Lifevest Publishing
Emotions of a Lifetime
4901 E. Dry Creek Road #170
Centennial, Colorado 80122